Sacha van Dulm

# The Stickleback

Barron's Woodbury, N.Y.

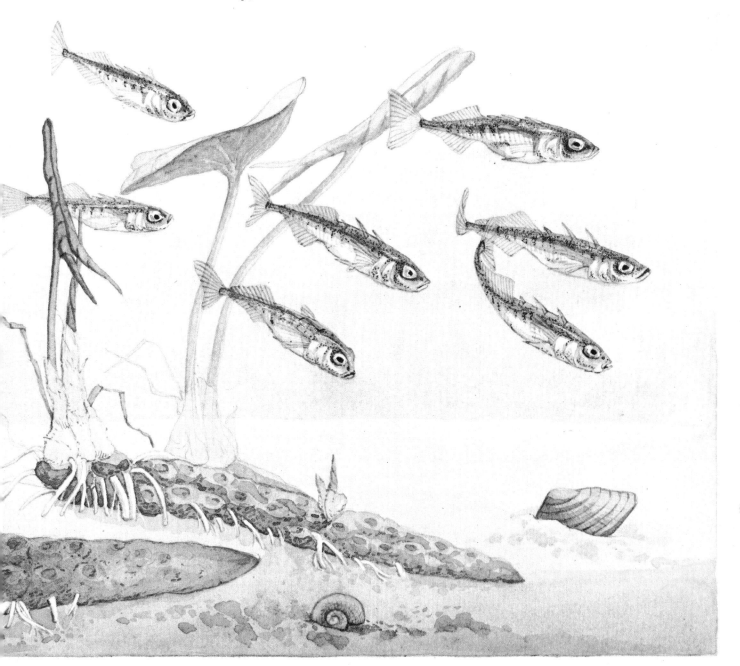

When spring comes, the stickle-backs travel by the thousands from the sea back to the old trusty canals where they came from in the fall. Their bodies easily adapt themselves so that now they can live in fresh water, too. They like to live in schools, so they can hunt for food together.

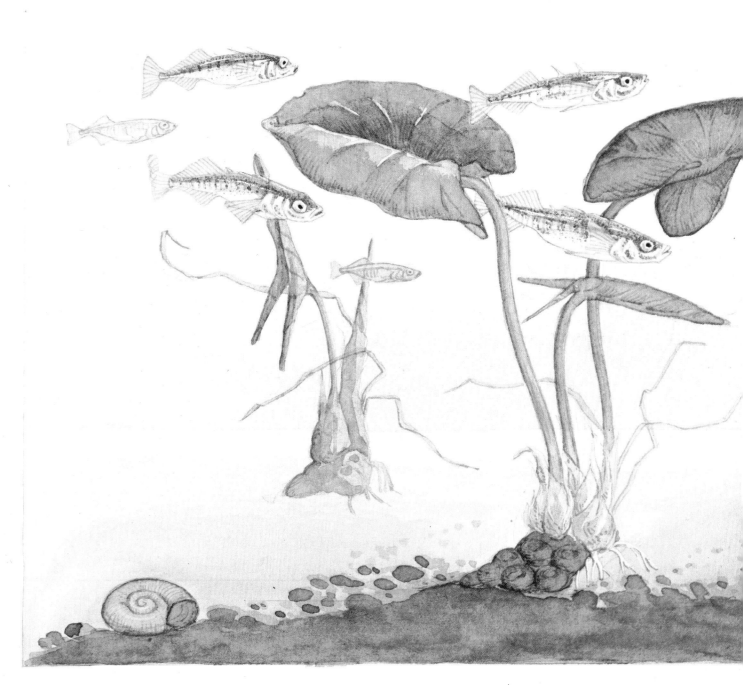

Whenever one finds something to eat, the others dash over like lightning to get some of the goodies. Failing that, they scour the area until they find a victim.

Sticklebacks look like friendly fish, but actually they are the terror of all the smaller inhabitants of the canal.

The stickleback has his ene-
mies, too. But there aren't many
of them.
Examples are the larvae of the
yellow-rimmed water beetle
and the pike. The stickleback
has to watch out for these
animals.

The pike is very hungry. Sud-
denly he rushes at the school
of sticklebacks.
Luckily, they had noticed the
threatening shadow hovering
over them just in time.

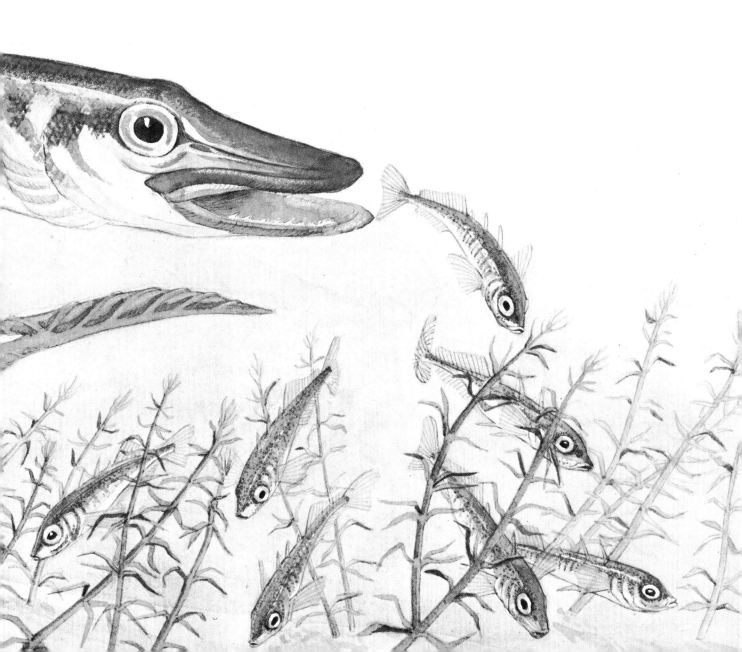

The heron standing stiffly at the waterside, patiently waiting his turn, saw everything. Two times now, this stickleback had been lucky, but now his luck had run out.
With a quick movement of his beak, the heron finishes him off. He swallows the fish, and once again stands motionless.

When spring comes, the males
change color.
The change begins with the
eyes, which become bright blue.
Then their stomachs get redder
and redder. Their backs
become a shiny blue-green
color.
Every stickleback has his own
territory, and woe to anyone
who intrudes!
Their spines stand on end,
and each one shows his red
stomach threateningly to any
challenger.

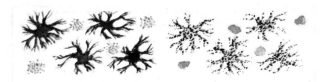

Now the male starts building his nest. It's very simple. He picks up a little sand and spits it out over to the side. This way, he makes a little hole. He fills up the hole with algae and pieces of other water plants.
As soon as he has brought together enough plants, he slides over them with his stomach.

At the same time, he secretes a sticky fluid, which he uses to stick the pieces of plants together. He keeps pressing them down and sticking them together until he has created a solid heap.
When he is satisfied with it, he bores a hole in it with his nose and creeps through it. He does this several times, just enough to make a good nest.

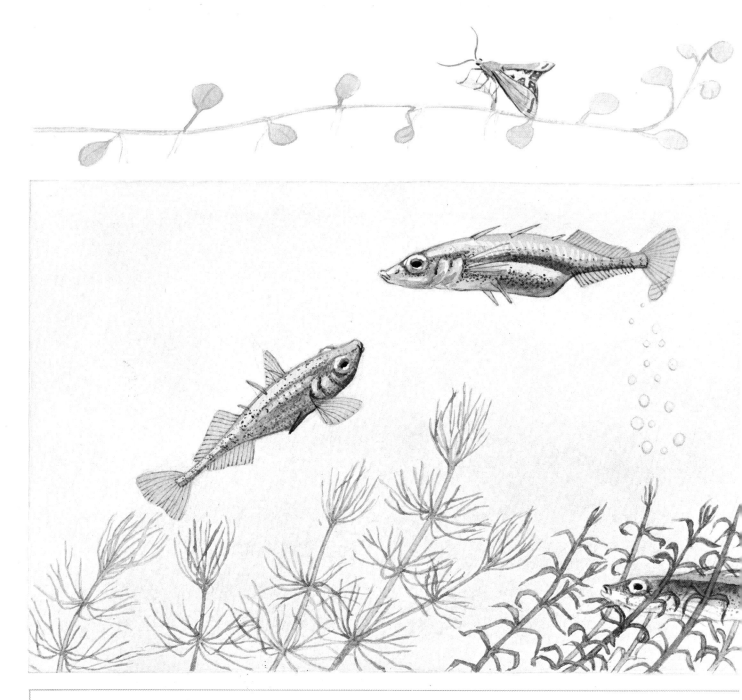

Meanwhile, his stomach has gotten a lot redder.
The color is attractive to a female that is full of eggs, but he chases them all.
He swims after them with quick, menacing zig-zag movements and with a wide-open mouth.

The females that are not yet filled with eggs run away quickly. Only a female that has a strong need to get rid of her eggs will not run. She will stay. She will turn her stomach toward the male. She will make quivering motions with her body. She will turn her head toward the male. We call this "mating".

This is how the male gets the female that is ready to mate.

Now the male swims back to his nest with quick, zig-zag motions. The female follows him.

He opens the nest with his mouth and shows her the entrance.

Having done that, he lies flat on one side. His whole body begins to shudder. This is her cue to come into the nest.

As soon as she is in the nest, the male gives her tail a little shove. Then later, she raises her tail, and the eggs come out by themselves.

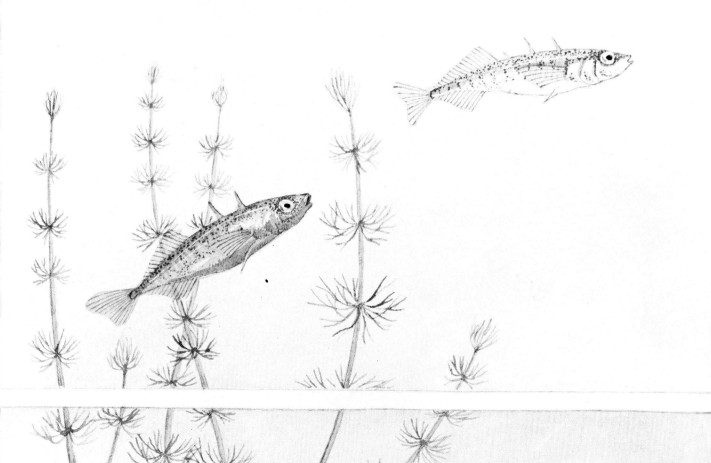

As soon as the female comes out of the nest, the male goes in. He sprays milt over the eggs to fertilize them. When that is done, he chases the female away. It is possible that she might eat her own eggs. Meanwhile, other females are in the vicinity.

The male spreads the eggs neatly over the bottom of the nest. The whole process might be repeated, only with different females.

When the nest is full, the male begins to take care of the eggs. He keeps his fins moving so that fresh water is constantly pushed over the eggs. After a week, the eggs hatch. The little fish grow quickly.

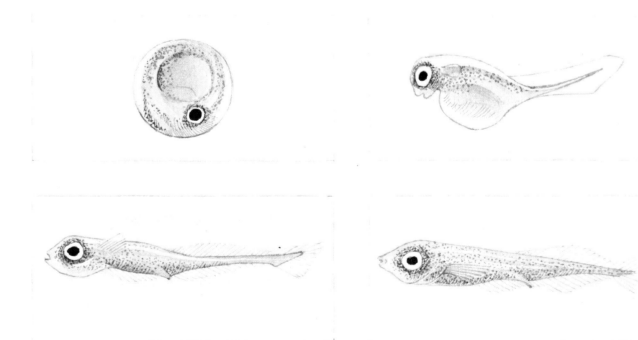

One day after their birth, the
little fish begin to swim around
in the vicinity of the nest.
The father has to watch care-
fully, because little sticklebacks
are a delicacy for all kinds of
other fish, even other stickle-
backs.
Whenever one of them gets out,
the father grabs him and spits
him back into the nest.

The father guards the little ones for one week. After that, he goes his own way. Completely unaware of the great danger they are in, the young stickle-backs swim around unsuspect-ingly.

The water shrew, the otter, the grebe, and the larvae of the yellow-rimmed water beetle all lie in wait, ready to appease their hunger.

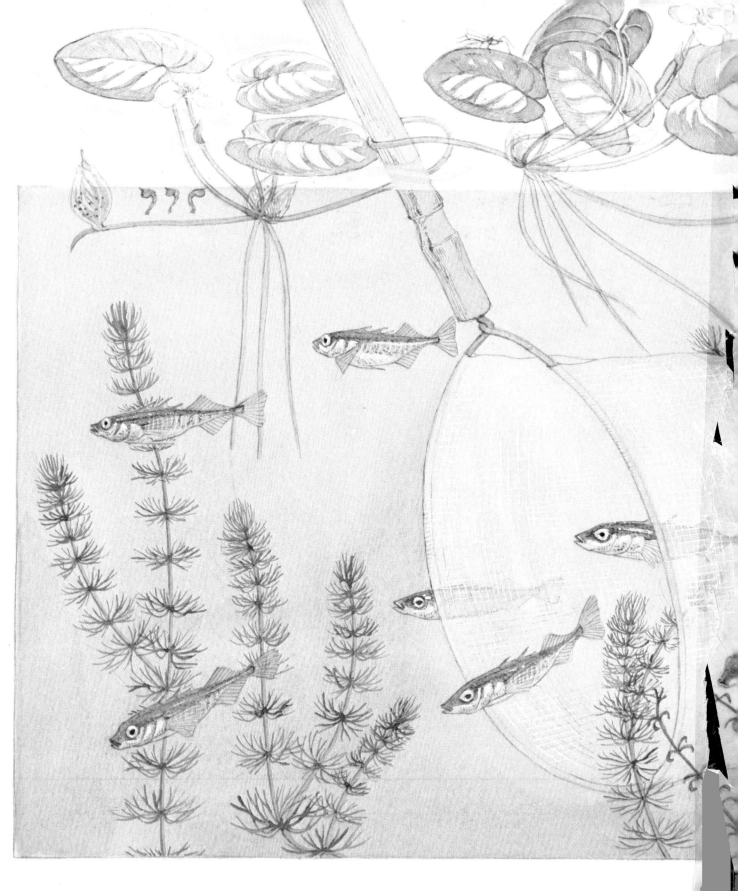

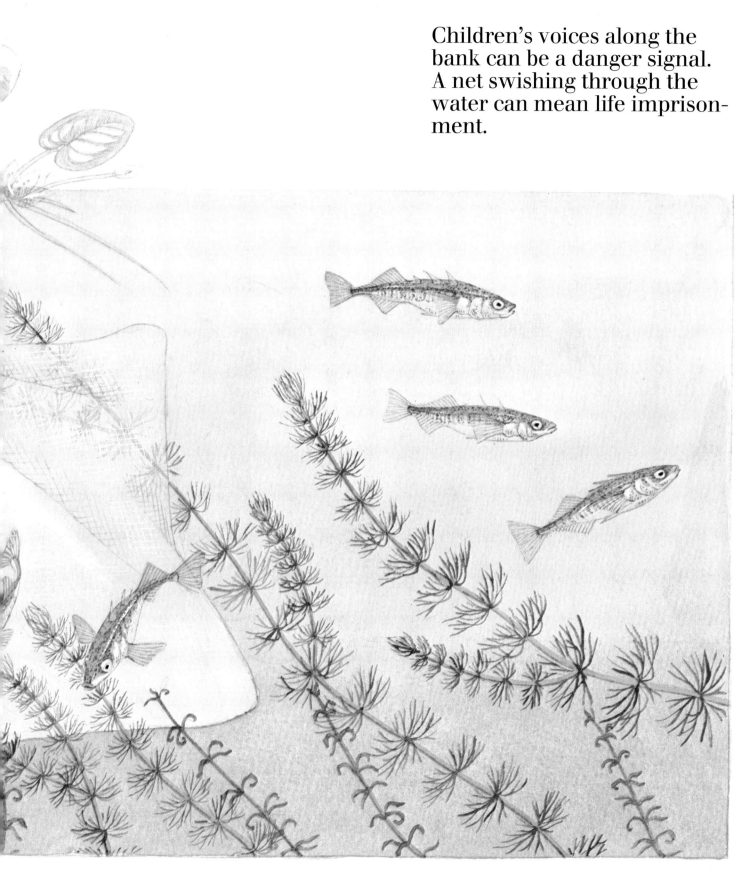

Children's voices along the bank can be a danger signal. A net swishing through the water can mean life imprisonment.

As the fall gets closer and the days grow shorter, the stickle-backs that remain gather together. They leave the canal and head out in the direction of the sea.

If it were possible, it would be interesting to see them swim.

They are going through the exact same canals as in the previous year. The young ones are doing it for the first time, the

older ones for the second or perhaps even the third time, but they all go out to sea to pass the winter there.

# THE WORLD'S TOP TEN

# LAKES

## Neil Morris

ILLUSTRATED BY VANESSA CARD

RSVP

RAINTREE
STECK-VAUGHN
PUBLISHERS
The Steck-Vaughn Company

*Austin, Texas*

Words in **bold** are explained in the glossary
on pages 30–31.

Text copyright © Neil Morris 1997
Illustrations copyright © Vanessa Card 1997
© Copyright 1997 Steck-Vaughn Company this edition

Published by Raintree Steck-Vaughn Publishers, an imprint
of Steck-Vaughn Company.

**Picture acknowledgements:**
J. Allan Cash: 16, 17, 24, 26, 27, 29t. James Davis
Photography: 5b, 28b, 29b. Eye Ubiquitous: 5t &11
© L. Fordyce, 15 © K. Mullineaux. First Light: 10 © Grant
Black, 14 © Alan Marsh. Lyn Hancock: 22, 23. Robert
Harding Picture Library: 18. Hutchison Picture Library:
8 © A. Grachtchenkov, 21 © Crispin Hughes. Link:
20 © Ron Gilrig. Novosti: 9. Panos: 19 © Marcus Rose.
Still Pictures: 13 © T. de Sallis, 25 © Hjalte Tiu. Trip:
12 © Johnson Hicks, 28t © Eric Smith.

**Editors:** Claire Edwards, Heather Luff
**Designer:** Dawn Apperley
**Picture researcher:** Diana Morris
**Consultant:** Elizabeth M. Lewis

**Library of Congress Cataloging-in-Publication Data**
Morris, Neil.
    Lakes / Neil Morris; illustrated by Vanessa Card.
      p.   cm. — (The world's top ten)
    Includes index.
    Summary: Presents information about the locations,
features, and other aspects of the world's ten largest lakes,
including Lake Superior, Lake Victoria, Lake Tanganyika,
and the Caspian Sea.
    ISBN 0-8172-4345-3
    1. Lakes — Juvenile literature. [1. Lakes.] I. Card,
Vanessa, ill. II. Title. III. Series.
GB1603.8.M67   1997
551.48'2 — dc20             96-27639
                         CIP  AC

Printed in China
Bound in the United States
1 2 3 4 5 6 7 8 9 0 LB 00 99 98 97 96

# Contents

# What Is a Lake?

A lake is a body of water that is surrounded by land. Lakes form in hollows in the Earth's surface called **basins**. Lakewater comes from rainfall and melting snow. Much of the water flows into the basin from rivers and streams. Most lakes are full of **freshwater**, but the biggest lake in the world is salty. Some lakes are so large they have been called seas.

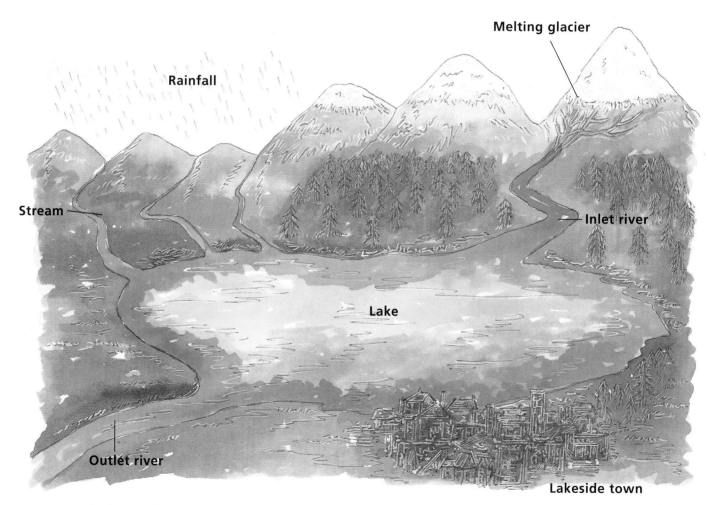

Melting glacier

Rainfall

Stream

Inlet river

Lake

Outlet river

Lakeside town

## How lakes form

Many lakes are in areas that were once occupied by masses of ice called **glaciers**. The glaciers made hollows in the ground as they moved. When the ice melted, these basins filled with water.

Other lake basins formed when the Earth's **crust** moved. **Volcanoes**, **earthquakes**, and widening cracks in the crust made large holes that filled with water from rivers or underground **springs**.

Crater Lake, in Oregon, formed when rain and melting snow filled the crater of a volcano thousands of years ago. The island in the lake is the tip of another, smaller volcano.

## Lake dwellers

We have learned a lot by digging up remains of **settlements** near lakes and finding out how ancient people lived. Thousands of years ago, people in Europe sometimes built houses over the water at the edge of lakes.

The houses were on wooden platforms that stood on posts driven into the **lakebed**. These early people lived by lakes because water and **transportation** were in good supply. In some parts of the world, people still live in stilt houses on lakes.

## The biggest lakes

In this book we will take a look at the ten biggest lakes in the world. We will see how different they are from each other and get to know the people and animals who have made lakes and lakeshores their homes.

The ancient town of Sirmione lies on the shores of Lake Garda, in northern Italy. **Ruins** of Roman houses have been found here, dating back more than 2,000 years.

# The Biggest Lakes

This map shows where the ten biggest lakes are in the world. These are the lakes with the largest surface area, measured in square miles. The biggest of all is the Caspian Sea, and it is a saltwater lake. It is more than four times bigger than Lake Superior, the next lake on the list. When you stand on the shores of the Caspian Sea, you cannot see the land on the other side so it looks more like the sea than a lake. Number nine in our list, Lake Baikal, is the world's deepest lake and holds the most freshwater.

### The World's Top Ten Lakes

| | | |
|---|---|---|
| **1** | Caspian Sea | 144,000 sq mi |
| **2** | Lake Superior | 31,800 sq mi |
| **3** | Lake Victoria | 26,800 sq mi |
| **4** | Lake Huron | 23,000 sq mi |
| **5** | Lake Michigan | 22,400 sq mi |
| **6** | Aral Sea | 14,300 sq mi |
| **7** | Lake Tanganyika | 12,700 sq mi |
| **8** | Great Bear Lake | 12,300 sq mi |
| **9** | Lake Baikal | 11,800 sq mi |
| **10** | Lake Malawi | 11,400 sq mi |

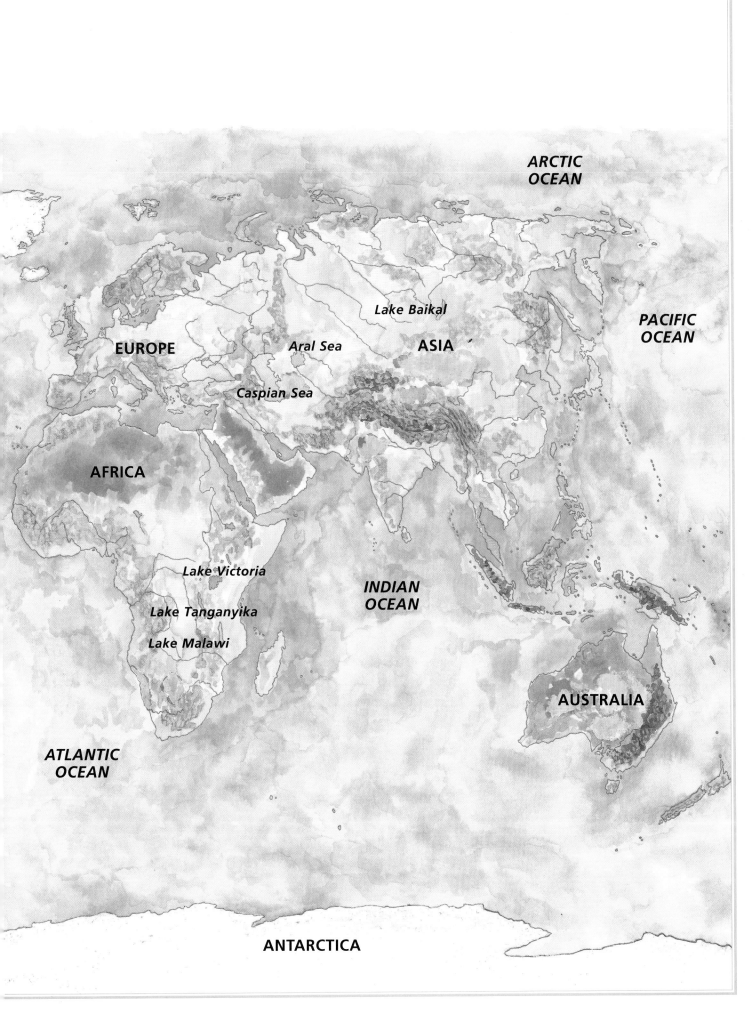

# Caspian Sea

The Caspian Sea is the largest lake in the world. Scientists believe that it is probably the world's oldest lake, too. Many rivers flow into this huge **saltwater** lake, including Europe's longest river, the Volga. But not a single river flows out of it.

Russian fishermen set their nets in the Volga River, trying to catch fish swimming to the Caspian Sea. The fishermen's most valuable catch is the sturgeon.

## Saltwater

The Volga River flows for over 2,200 miles (3,500 km) before it empties into the Caspian Sea. Near the Volga **delta**, the lake's water is almost free of salt. Most of the lake's water is less salty than normal seawater. But in the shallow **gulf** called Kara-Bogaz-Gol, the water is ten times as salty as seawater. There the lakebed is covered by a layer of salt 7 feet (2 m) thick.

## Between Europe and Asia

The Ural Mountains form the border between the **continents** of Europe and Asia. At the southern end of the mountains, the Ural River flows to the Caspian Sea. The lake's eastern and southern shores belong to Kazakhstan, Turkmenistan, and Iran.

The western and northern shores belong to Azerbaijan, Russia, and Kazakhstan. The land surrounding the lake ranges form the Caucasus and Elburz Mountains to the Karagiye Depressions. The surface of the lake lies 92 feet (28 m) below **sea level**.

### FACTS

AREA   143,600 square miles (371,800 sq km)

GREATEST LENGTH   761 miles (1,225 km)

GREATEST DEPTH   3,400 feet (1,025 m)

ALTITUDE   –92 feet (–28 m)

LOCATION   Azerbaijan, Iran, Russia, Kazakhstan, Turkmenistan

The wind has whipped up the Caspian Sea so that surf breaks on the shores of Turkmenistan. This makes the world's largest lake look like an ocean.

## Oil production

Once the Caspian was famous for caviar, the **roe** of the sturgeon. But fishing and industrial **pollution** have reduced the number of fish in the lake. Now the lake's most important **resources** are oil and natural gas. Companies drill for oil on the shore and beneath the waters of the lake. The countries along the Caspian want to increase their oil production, but many people are worried that the lake could become more polluted.

# Lake Superior

Lake Superior is the biggest and deepest of the five Great Lakes of North America, and it is the largest freshwater lake in the world. The lake lies on the border between the United States and Canada, and the **national boundary** runs right across it.

CANADA

Minnesota

Red fox

Isle Royale

Moose

Beaver

Forest

CANADA

U.S.

Fishing

Walleye

Otter

Duluth

ONTARIO

*St. Louis River*

Yellow perch

Wisconsin

Deer

*St. Marys River*

Michigan

Sault Sainte Marie

UNITED STATES

*Lake Michigan*

*Lake Huron*

## Upper lake

Long before Europeans arrived in North America, Ojibwa and Menominee Indian tribes lived around the lakeshores. The Ojibwa used birch bark to build **wigwams** and canoes and lived on otter, beaver, and fish from the lake. In 1622 the French explorer, Étienne Brûlé, reached the lake, and he was later followed by fur **traders**. They called the lake Lac Supérieur, which means Upper Lake.

Icy waves break on the Canadian shore of Lake Superior. The lake does not completely freeze over in winter, but the **harbors** are usually iced over for at least three months.

A ship enters one of the Soo Canal locks, where the water level is lowered and raised to let ships pass through.

**FACTS**
AREA    31,800 square miles (82,350 sq km)
GREATEST LENGTH    350 miles (560 km)
GREATEST DEPTH    1,330 feet (406 m)
ALTITUDE    600 feet (183 m)
LOCATION    Canada, U.S.

## Flowing in and out

About two hundred rivers flow into Lake Superior. The largest is the St. Louis River at the western end of the lake. At the eastern end, the lake flows into the St. Marys River, which links it to Lake Huron, the fourth biggest lake in the world. Lake Superior lies 600 feet (183 m) above sea level, which is 23 feet (7 m) higher than Lake Huron. To avoid **rapids** on St. Marys River, ships pass through the five **locks** of the Soo Canals at the twin cities of Sault Sainte Marie.

## Rocky shores and islands

Lake Superior is surrounded by a rocky coastline and beautiful forests. At Pictured Rocks National Lakeshore, in Michigan, multicolored sandstone cliffs rise up to 200 feet (60 m) for a stretch of 15 miles (24 km). Wind and rain have carved the cliffs into strange shapes. The lake's largest island, Isle Royale, is a U.S. **national park**. Beavers, snowshoe hares, and red foxes live on the island.

11

# Lake Victoria

Victoria is the largest lake in Africa and the third largest lake in the world. Lake Victoria has the highest **altitude** of the world's top ten lakes. It lies on the **Equator** and is divided mainly between the countries of Uganda and Tanzania. A small part of its waters and shoreline belong to Kenya.

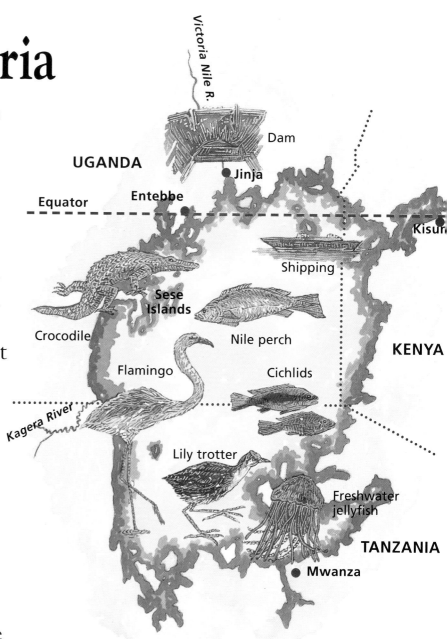

Victoria Nile R.

UGANDA

Dam

Jinja

Equator

Entebbe

Kisu

Shipping

Sese Islands

Nile perch

KENYA

Crocodile

Flamingo

Cichlids

Kagera River

Lily trotter

Freshwater jellyfish

TANZANIA

Mwanza

## Source of the Nile

In 1858 an English explorer, John Hanning Speke, went in search of the **source** of the Nile River, the longest river in the world. He came across a huge lake that he named Lake Victoria in honor of Queen Victoria. We now know that the true source of the Nile is a branch of the Kagera, one of the many rivers that flow into Lake Victoria. The Nile is the only river that flows out of the lake.

Lake Victoria is the shallowest of the large freshwater lakes and contains many small islands. These are the Sese Islands off the Ugandan coast.

The Owen Falls **Dam** was built across the Victoria Nile River, near Jinja. When it opened in 1954, the dam raised the level of Lake Victoria by almost three feet. The dam is used to make electricity.

## On a high plateau

The lake's surface is more than 3,280 feet (1,000 m) above sea level. The lake's waters fill a shallow basin on a high **plateau** that formed about 750,000 years ago. This area of high land lies between two deep valleys. The valleys are part of the long series of deep cracks in the Earth's surface known as the **Great Rift Valley**.

**FACTS**

AREA   26,800 square miles (69,500 sq km)
GREATEST LENGTH   224 miles (360 km)
GREATEST DEPTH   270 feet (82 m)
ALTITUDE   3,720 feet (1,135 m)
LOCATION   Kenya, Tanzania, Uganda

## Major ports

Millions of people live near the shores of Lake Victoria. Shipping services link the main ports of three countries: Mwanza in Tanzania, Entebbe in Uganda, and Kisumu in Kenya. The lake is a valuable source of fish and contains 170 kinds of **tropical** fish called cichlids. Many small fish have been killed off by the Nile perch, which was introduced into the lake in 1964.

# Lake Huron

Lake Huron is the second largest of the Great Lakes in North America. The border between the United States and Canada runs across the lake. Water flows into the lake from Lake Superior, down the St. Marys River, and from Lake Michigan, through the **Straits** of Mackinac. Water also flows in from other small rivers.

## The Huron people

Lake Huron was the first of the Great Lakes to be discovered by Europeans. A French explorer named Samuel de Champlain reached the lake in 1615 and found Huron Indians living on its shores. French fur traders followed Champlain to the lake and named it after the native people.

*Lake Superior*

Deer

**CANADA**

*St. Marys River*

*Lake Michigan*

**Straits of Mackinac**

Black bear

**Manitoulin**

Lake trout

Chipmun

**UNITED STATES**

CANADA
U.S.

*Georgian Bay*

Beaver

**Michigan**

Belted kingfisher

Pine forest

Shipping

Raccoon

Silver maple

**Port Huron** ●

● **Sarnia**

*St. Clair River*

Forests grow along the shore of Lake Huron in Ontario, Canada. Before Europeans arrived the Huron people lived in villages in lakeside forests of blue beech, white pine, and silver maple.

## FACTS

AREA    23,000 square miles
(59,600 sq km)

GREATEST LENGTH    205 miles (330 km)

GREATEST DEPTH    750 feet (229 m)

ALTITUDE    577 feet (176 m)

LOCATION    Canada, U.S.

## Saint Lawrence Seaway

Lake Huron and the other Great Lakes form part of a waterway that allows ships to sail over 2,300 miles (3,700 km) from the Atlantic Ocean to the port of Duluth on Lake Superior. This waterway is called the St. Lawrence Seaway. Ice on the lakes usually stops shipping from January to March each year.

## Large islands

Like all the Great Lakes and most lakes around the world, Huron is dotted with islands. Most lie in the northern part of the lake, especially in Georgian Bay. The two biggest islands are Mackinac, in the American section of the lake, and Manitoulin, on the Canadian side. Manitoulin is the largest island in freshwater in the world. It is 80 miles (129 km) long and is covered in forest. The Manitoulin islanders make a living from tourism as well as timber.

This group of Georgian Bay islands form a national park. The forests and wildlife in national parks are protected. Some small towns can be seen from the air.

15

# Lake Michigan

Lake Michigan is the third largest of the Great Lakes in North America. It lies entirely within the United States and is bordered by four different states: Michigan to the north and east, Wisconsin to the west, and Illinois and Indiana to the south.

This marina, on the shores of Lake Michigan outside of Chicago, is a place where tourists and local people enjoy boating for leisure.

## European explorers

Menominee and other Indian tribes lived near the shores of the lake long before European explorers and fur-traders arrived. A Frenchman, Jean Nicolet, was the first European to reach the area in 1634. He set out to explore the lake believing that he would end up in China. When his canoe reached land, he went ashore wearing a Chinese robe. Instead he had landed on the Wisconsin side of Lake Michigan, the home of Native Americans.

A lakeside view of Chicago shows some of the tallest buildings in the world. The modern **skyscraper** was invented in this great city.

## City ports

All four states around the lake have large, busy ports. Milwaukee, the chief port and industrial center of Wisconsin, has a population of 1.6 million. The biggest lakeside port of all is Chicago, in Illinois, which is the third largest city in the United States, with a population of 8 million. The city is divided by the Chicago River, which flows out of the lake. The Chicago and Illinois rivers, together with the Chicago Sanitary and Ship Canal, link Lake Michigan to the Mississippi River.

**FACTS**

AREA    23,400 square miles
(58,000 sq km)

GREATEST LENGTH   307 miles (494 km)

GREATEST DEPTH   922 feet (281 m)

ALTITUDE   577 feet (176 m)

LOCATION   U.S.

## Sleeping Bear Dunes

On the other side of the lake, there is a towering mass of sand dunes. These dunes cover 30 miles (50 km) of shoreline, and some are 440 feet (135 m) high. This part of Michigan is now protected. It is called Sleeping Bear Dunes National Lakeshore. The name comes from a huge hill of sand that is shaped like a bear at rest.

17

# Aral Sea

The Aral Sea lies about 250 miles (400 km) east of the Caspian Sea, between Uzbekistan and Kazakhstan. It has slipped from fourth to sixth on the list of the world's largest lakes because it is shrinking. Water from the rivers that feed the lake has been diverted into constructed canals. Every year the lake's water level drops, and its shoreline moves back a little more.

KAZAKHASTAN

Irrigated area

Syr Darya R

Goat

Sheep

Herdsman

Great bustard

Muynak

Gas

Muskrat

Irrigated area

Darkling beetle

Amu Darya River

Oil

Cotton

UZBEKISTAN

The Amu Darya River flows through Uzbekistan towards the Aral Sea. Today its waters scarcely reach the shrinking lake.

## Sea of islands

The Aral Sea's name means "sea of islands." Just 30 years ago, the Aral contained over 1,100 small islands. Many of these have now joined together as the water level drops. The lake's water comes from two rivers, the Amu Darya and the Syr Darya. In 1980 the Karakumsky Canal was opened. This canal takes water from the Amu Darya hundreds of miles before the river reaches the Aral Sea. The water is used to help desert people in Turkmenistan irrigate their cotton fields.

## Desert sea

The Karakumsky Canal and other **irrigation** projects have helped farmers in some areas, but they have made the land around the Aral Sea a desert. Fishing villages that were on the shoreline of the lake 30 years ago are now many miles from its shores. The land between the villages and the lake has dried up, leaving behind huge amounts of salt. Nothing will grow there. The lake and surrounding areas are very polluted. Many fishing boats are just rotting away.

### FACTS

AREA   14,300 square miles (37,000 sq km)

GREATEST LENGTH   218 miles (350 km)

GREATEST DEPTH   223 feet (68 m)

ALTITUDE   174 feet (53 m)

LOCATION   Kazakhstan, Uzbekistan

This boat is one of many left stranded in the desert when the Aral shoreline moved away from the port of Muynak.

## Changing nature

Just a few years ago, the Aral Sea was teeming with fish. Now there is no fishing harvest and at least 24 species of Aral fish have died out. In the 1970s some people wanted to divert bigger Russian rivers to the area to make up for the water already lost. But scientists realized that this would only make the situation worse. There are now international discussions to try to solve the Aral region's problems.

# Lake Tanganyika

Tanganyika, in East Africa, is the seventh largest and second deepest lake in the world. It is the world's longest freshwater lake at 450 miles (725 km), yet its widest point is only 45 miles (72 km). The border between Zaire and Tanzania runs through the lake, with small parts of its shoreline belonging to Burundi and Zambia.

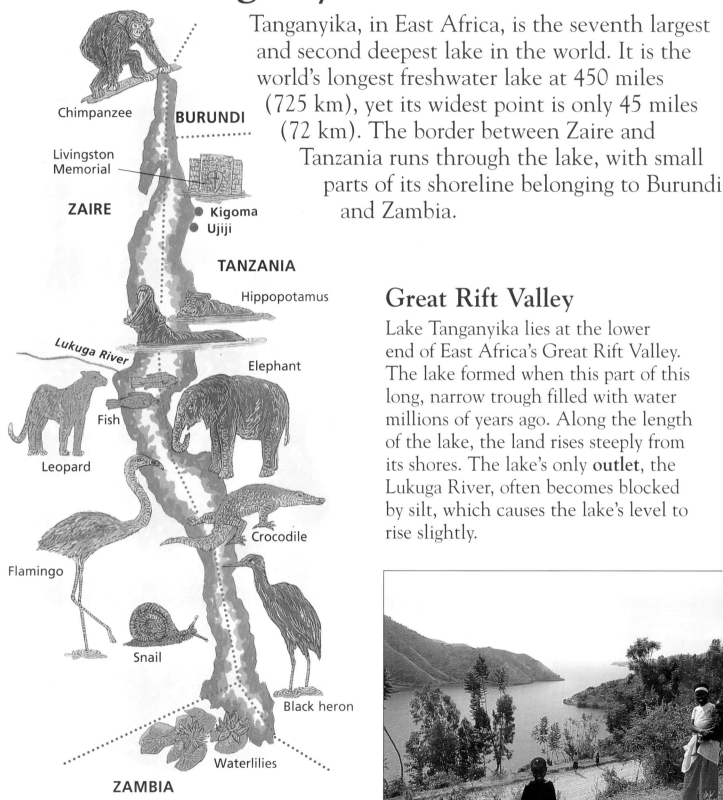

Chimpanzee

BURUNDI

Livingston Memorial

ZAIRE

Kigoma

Ujiji

TANZANIA

Hippopotamus

Lukuga River

Elephant

Fish

Leopard

Crocodile

Flamingo

Snail

Black heron

Waterlilies

ZAMBIA

## Great Rift Valley

Lake Tanganyika lies at the lower end of East Africa's Great Rift Valley. The lake formed when this part of this long, narrow trough filled with water millions of years ago. Along the length of the lake, the land rises steeply from its shores. The lake's only **outlet**, the Lukuga River, often becomes blocked by silt, which causes the lake's level to rise slightly.

Local people live on the hillsides near the lake in Burundi. In recent years a terrible war has been fought by the different peoples of this country.

## Stanley and Livingstone

African tribes have lived near the lakeshores for thousands of years. The first Europeans to find Lake Tanganyika were Sir Richard Burton and John Hanning Speke in 1858. They reached Ujiji, on the eastern shore, while searching for the source of the Nile River. In 1869 Henry Morton Stanley went in search of the Scottish explorer David Livingstone, who had been missing. After a difficult journey, Stanley found Livingstone in 1871 at Ujiji and greeted him with the words, "Doctor Livingstone, I presume?"

Kigoma, Tanzania's main port on the lake, is just 5 miles (8 km) from the old fishing village of Ujiji. Today timber, cotton, and tobacco are shipped from Kigoma.

### FACTS
AREA   12,700 square miles (32,900 sq km)

GREATEST LENGTH   451 miles (725 km)

GREATEST DEPTH   4,708 feet (1,435 m)

ALTITUDE   2,533 feet (772 m)

LOCATION   Burundi, Tanzania, Zaire, Zambia

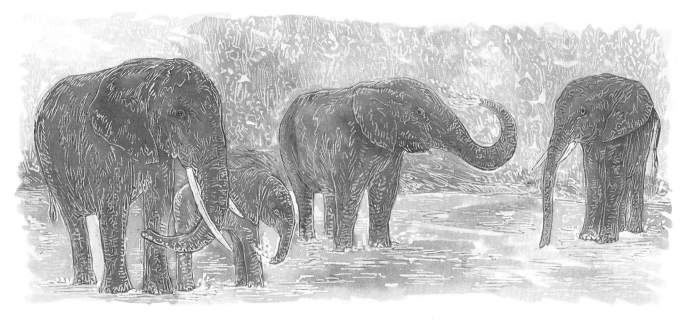

## Rich wildlife

Many of Lake Tanganyika's fish are not found anywhere else in the world. This has happened because the lake is very old and has remained separate from other bodies of water for a long time. Tanganyika is also home to hippopotamuses, crocodiles, and large numbers of water birds. African elephants roam through the surrounding forests, and troops of chimpanzees live in the nearby **rain forest** of Zaire. The lake's beauty and wildlife attract tourists from all over the world.

# Great Bear Lake

Great Bear Lake, in the Northwest Territories of Canada, is the most northern of the world's largest lakes. It lies on the Arctic Circle, and it is fed by melting snow. The lake drains into the Great Bear River, a tributary of the Mackenzie River, which flows into the Arctic Ocean.

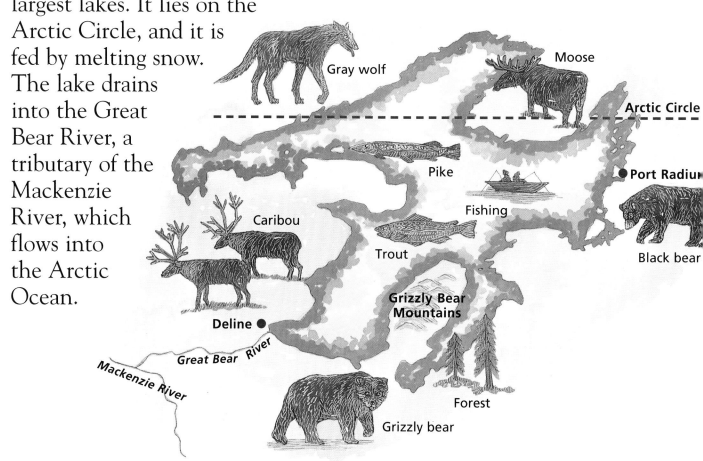

Gray wolf

Moose

Arctic Circle

Pike

Port Radium

Fishing

Caribou

Trout

Black bear

Grizzly Bear Mountains

Deline

Great Bear River

Mackenzie River

Forest

Grizzly bear

GREAT BEAR LAKE
ICE CROSSING
OPEN
MAX. G.V.W.
50000kg.

MAXIMUM
20

## In the far north

Great Bear Lake's climate is cold, and the lake is free from ice for only four months of the year. It is surrounded by the northern edge of Canada's taiga, a huge forest of evergreen trees. The first people to live here were Native American people called the Dene. In the Dene language, the lake is called Sahtu, meaning "bear water."

This crossing, at the edge of the lake near Deline, is open during the coldest months when the ice is very thick. It connects with a normal road.

## Fishing and mining

Great Bear Lake is famous for fishing. The world's largest lake trout was caught here in 1991. It weighed more than 66 pounds (30 kg). Great Bear Lake has many other fish, too, such as pike, grayling, and whitefish. Visitors need a fishing **license** to fish here, and they return the catch to the lake after weighing it. Port Radium, on the eastern shore, was named for the pitchblende, containing radium and uranium, once mined there. The mines are now closed.

These houses are fishing lodges on an island in Great Bear Lake. They are open to fishing visitors and other vacationers during the summer months.

### FACTS

AREA    12,300 square miles
        (31,800 sq km)

GREATEST LENGTH    232 miles (373 km)

GREATEST DEPTH    1,348 feet (411 m)

ALTITUDE    390 feet (119 m)

LOCATION    Canada

## Arctic wildlife

The black bears and grizzlies that gave the lake its name still roam the area today. Black bears live in the forest and lowland areas, while grizzlies prefer the nearby mountains. The region's other large animals are moose and caribou. Moose have always been very important to the Sahtu Dene people, providing them with meat and hides, as well as bones and antlers for tools. Bald eagles and golden eagles are also found in the region.

# Lake Baikal

Lake Baikal lies in southeastern Russia, just north of Mongolia. It is the deepest lake in the world, and holds more water than any other freshwater lake. More than one-fifth of the world's fresh water is in this lake. With 336 rivers flowing into it, Baikal has just one outlet, the Angara River. This is a **tributary** of the Yenisei, the fifth longest river in the world.

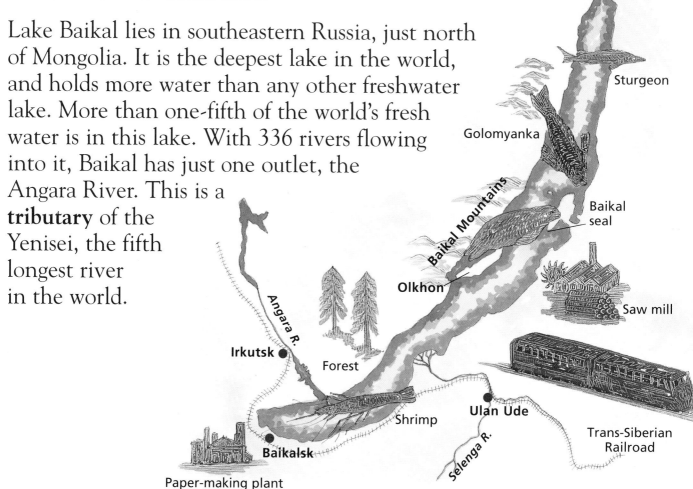

Sturgeon

Golomyanka

Baikal Mountains

Baikal seal

Olkhon

Saw mill

Angara R.

Irkutsk

Forest

Shrimp

Ulan Ude

Trans-Siberian Railroad

Baikalsk

Selenga R.

Paper-making plant

Ships are stuck once the lake has frozen in January. The ice can be more than 5 feet (1.5 m) thick in places, and sometimes it cracks with a loud bang.

## People of Baikal

The Baikal region is the traditional homeland of the Buryat people, and their land, Buryatia, forms one of Russia's 22 republics. The Buryats were once nomads, moving their felt tents around the southern shores of the lake. Now they almost all live in wooden houses, especially during winter. The lake freezes during winter months, and people fish through holes in the ice.

## Unique seals and fish

Lake Baikal is about 25 million years old and is home to some amazing species of wildlife that are not found anywhere else on Earth. The world's smallest and only freshwater seal, the Baikal seal, lives here. The lake also contains many fish, including huge sturgeon that grow longer than the small seals. An unusual species of deepwater fish called golomyanka, or Baikal cod, is also found here. Unlike most fish, the Baikal cod gives birth to live young rather than laying eggs. In addition Lake Baikal contains one-third of the world's freshwater shrimps.

## Siberian industry

Baikal's water was once famous in Russia for being clear and pure. Visitors came to drink and bathe in the lake. In recent years, however, industry has developed around the lake, and pollution is now an increasing problem.

The paper-making plants, saw mills, shipbuilders, and fish-processing factories are a threat to the lake **environment**. Local and other people are working to protect Lake Baikal, the world's largest body of fresh water.

This factory, on the southern shores of the lake at Baikalsk, processes pulp for making paper. Protesters have tried to stop the factory from polluting the lake with its waste.

### FACTS

AREA   11,800 square miles (30,500 sq km)

GREATEST LENGTH   385 miles (620 km)

GREATEST DEPTH   5,315 feet (1,620 m)

ALTITUDE   1,493 feet (455 m)

LOCATION   Russia

25

# Lake Malawi

Most of Lake Malawi, sometimes called Nyasa, lies within the East African country of Malawi. Some of the lake's waters belong to neighboring Mozambique, and the border of Tanzania runs along its northeastern shoreline. The lake is fed by 14 rivers and has one outlet, the Shire River, which joins the bigger Zambezi River and flows to the Indian Ocean.

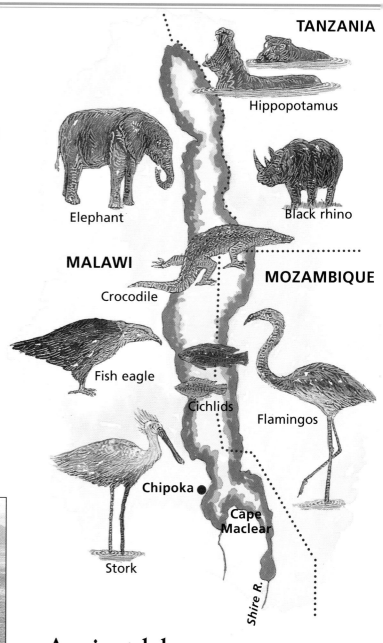

TANZANIA

Hippopotamus

Elephant

Black rhino

MALAWI

MOZAMBIQUE

Crocodile

Fish eagle

Cichlids

Flamingos

Chipoka

Cape Maclear

Stork

Shire R.

## Ancient lake

Malawi is the third largest lake of the Great Rift Valley, after Victoria and Tanganyika. Fossils found in the region show that there has been a lake here for 120 million years ago. The present lake is more than 2,300 feet (700 m) deep. Today seasonal changes in rainfall cause the level of the lake to rise and fall slightly. During heavy rain the lake fills up and prevents flooding. In the dry season, the lake continues releasing water and keeps the rivers from drying up.

This rocky inlet is at Cape Maclear, which juts into the southern end of Lake Malawi.

The choppy waves in Lake Malawi are created by high winds blowing over the surface of the lake. The waves make Lake Malawi look like the open sea.

## Lake of storms

When explorer David Livingstone reached the lake in 1859, he asked the local African people what it was called. They replied "Nyasa," meaning "lake," and so Livingstone named it Lake Nyasa. Later the country that formed around its shores was called Nyasaland.

In 1964 the country's name changed to Malawi, which means "broad water." Livingstone once also called Lake Malawi the "lake of storms." From May to August, a southeasterly wind often blows into a gale and creates high waves, making it look like the open sea.

**FACTS**

AREA   11,400 square miles (29,600 sq km)

GREATEST LENGTH   360 miles (580 km)

GREATEST DEPTH   2,300 feet (701 m)

ALTITUDE   1,550 feet (472 m)

LOCATION   Malawi, Mozambique, Tanzania

## Fishing and sailing

Bantu tribes lived around the shores of Lake Malawi long before European explorers arrived. They lived on fish that they caught in the lake by using small boats. The lake has 200 different species of tropical cichlid fish. Today the fishing industry is based at the southern end of the lake. Passenger and cargo ships connect with the railroad at Chipoka. The ships carry cotton, rubber, rice, and peanuts, as well as fish.

# The World's Lakes

The world's biggest lake, the Caspian Sea, lies between Europe and Asia. The remaining nine lakes are found on three continents—four in North America, three in Africa, and two in Asia. But there are important lakes on the other continents too, and they are also very different from each other.

## Lake Eyre, Australia

Australia's largest lake does not usually have any water in it. The **desert** lands of South Australia are so hot and dry that Lake Eyre (right) is normally a huge area of mud covered with a crust of salt. This salt lake covers an area of 3,430 square miles (8900 sq km) In years that have very heavy rainfall, the lake fills with water. This has happened four times since 1950.

## Lake Geneva, France and Switzerland

This is the largest of the lakes in the European Alps and has an area of 223 square miles (577 sq km). Lake Geneva's northern shore is in Switzerland, and its southern shore is in France. The Rhône River enters the lake at one end and flows out at the other, on its way from the mountains to the Mediterranean Sea. The lakeside Swiss city of Geneva (left) was founded by the Romans. Its fountain shoots a spray of water 476 feet (145 m) above the surface of the lake.

# Lake Titicaca, Peru and Bolivia

This large South American lake (right) lies in the Andes Mountains on the border between Peru and Bolivia. At 12,503 feet (3,811 m) above sea level, it is the highest **navigable** lake in the world. Its shores and islands are home to the Aymara people, who live by farming and fishing on the lake using reed boats.

# Loch Ness, Scotland

This long, narrow lake lies in a valley formed by a fault that runs across Scotland. Loch Ness is 23 miles (37 km) long and 2 miles (3 km) across.

This lake is famous for the monster in its deep waters that people claim to have seen. But all efforts to track down the monster have failed.

# Glossary

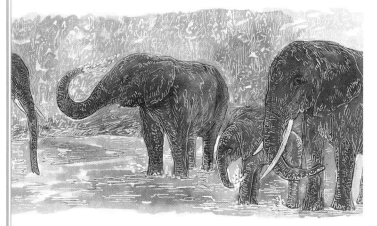

Elephants living in the continent of Africa.

**altitude**  Height above sea level

**basin**  A low area of land where a river or lake forms

**continent**  One of the Earth's huge land masses

**crust**  The Earth's outer shell

**dam**  A barrier built across a river, often used to make electricity

**delta**  The fan-shaped area at the mouth of some rivers

**desert**  A dry area of land where very little rain falls

**earthquake**  Movements in the Earth's crust that make the ground shake. Earthquakes can cause great damage.

**environment**  The surroundings in which people, animals, and plants live

**Equator**  An imaginary circle around the middle of the Earth

**freshwater**  Water that is not salty. Rainwater and riverwater are fresh.

**glacier**  A mass of ice that moves slowly like a river

**Great Rift Valley**  A long series of deep valleys in East Africa caused by cracks in the Earth's surface

**gulf**  A stretch of water with a wide, curving shoreline

**harbor**  A sheltered place where ships load and unload cargo

**irrigation**  A way of watering the land by means of canals and ditches

**lakebed**  The bottom of a lake

Baikal seals playing in the water.

**license**  A certificate that gives you permission to do something, such as fish

**lock**  Part of a canal or river that is closed off by gates so that the water level can be raised and lowered to let ships pass through

**mineral**  A solid substance that occurs naturally in the earth

**national boundary**  The border between different countries

**national park** An area that people may visit where animals and plants are protected

**navigable** A body of water big and deep enough for large boats to sail on

**outlet** River into which the water from a lake flows

**plateau** A flat area of high land

**pollution** Damage caused by poisonous and harmful substances

**rain forest** Thick forest found in warm tropical areas of heavy rainfall

**rapids** Part of a river where the water moves very fast over rocks

**resource** Something that people use to live or that can bring wealth when sold to others

**roe** Fish eggs (caviar)

**ruins** Buildings from long ago that have fallen down and decayed

**saltwater** Water with a concentration of salt, like the world's oceans and seas

**sea level** The sea's surface, used as the level from which to measure heights above and depths below; some land and lakes are below sea level

Tropical fish swimming in Lake Malawi.

**settlement** A place where people settle and live together

**skyscraper** A very high building

**source** The place where a river begins

**spring** A flow of water that comes bubbling out of the ground to form a stream

**strait** A narrow stretch of water between two areas of land

**trader** A person who buys and sells goods

**transportation** Ways of carrying people and goods from one place to another

**tributary** A small river that flows into a larger one

**tropical** Found in the tropics, the hottest part of the Earth near the Equator

**volcano** An opening where molten rock and gas come from deep inside the Earth, often forming a mountain.

**wigwam** A house made of bark, reeds, or skins spread over wooden poles. It usually looks like a tent

Sand dunes at Sleeping Bear National Park.

# Index

Words in **bold** appear in the glossary on pages 30-31.